Exploring World Cultures

Philippines

Joanne Mattern

WITHDRAWN

Cavendish
Square

New York

Published in 2018 by Cavendish Square Publishing, LLC
243 5th Avenue, Suite 136, New York, NY 10016

Copyright © 2018 by Cavendish Square Publishing, LLC

First Edition

Library of Congress Cataloging-in-Publication Data

Names: Mattern, Joanne, 1963- author.
Title: Philippines / Joanne Mattern.
Description: New York : Cavendish Square Publishing, [2018] |
Series: Exploring world cultures | Includes bibliographical references and index.
Identifiers: LCCN 2017015325 (print) | LCCN 2017016304 (ebook) | ISBN 9781502630193 (pbk.) | ISBN 9781502630216 (library bound) | ISBN 9781502630209 (6 pack) |
ISBN 9781502630223 (E-book)
Subjects: LCSH: Philippines--Juvenile literature.
Classification: LCC DS655 (ebook) | LCC DS655 .M387 2018 (print) |
DDC 959.9--dc23
LC record available at https://lccn.loc.gov/2017015325

Editorial Director: David McNamara
Editor: Kristen Susienka
Copy Editor: Alex Tessman
Associate Art Director: Amy Greenan
Designer: Graham Abbott
Production Coordinator: Karol Szymczuk
Photo Research: J8 Media

Contents

Introduction

The Philippines is a country in the southwestern Pacific Ocean. It is located on a chain of over seven thousand islands. These islands have high mountains, rolling farmland, and sandy beaches.

More than 102 million people live in the Philippines. The country has many crowded cities. Other people live in the countryside. There are more than one hundred different **ethnic** groups living in the Philippines.

The Philippines has had a long history. There have been violent and dangerous times in its past. Over the years, the Philippines has been ruled by other nations. It became independent in 1946, but faced many challenges.

The people of the Philippines are called Filipinos. Many say they are the friendliest people in the world. Filipinos enjoy sports and games. They eat tasty foods and spend time with their friends and families. The Philippines is a nation that is not like any other place in the world.

Shoppers jam a crowded street in Manila. It is one of the most crowded cities in the world.

Geography

The Philippines has 7,107 islands. The Philippines covers 120,000 square miles (310,000 square kilometers). It is the sixty-fourth largest country in the world.

This map shows the Philippines.

The largest island in the Philippines is called Luzon. Luzon lies in the northern part of the Philippines. The second-largest island is Mindanao, in the south.

Most of the Philippine islands have high mountains. The two highest mountains are on Mindanao. Mount Apo is 9,692 feet (2,954 meters). Mount Dulang-dulang is 9,649 feet (2,941 m).

A Land in Three Parts

The Philippines is divided into three parts. These parts are called Luzon, Visayas, and Mindanao.

Over the years, people have cut **terraces** into the lower parts of the mountains. They farm on these terraces. Farther down, the land is made of up flat grasslands, called plains. The coast of the Philippines is covered with beautiful beaches.

Mount Apo on Mindanao

The Philippines has one of the longest coastlines in the world.

7

The first people in
the Philippines came
from southeast Asia
thousands of years ago.
They hunted and fished.
Later, they farmed rice.

Ferdinand and Imelda Marcos at an official ceremony in 1984

After the 900s,
Filipinos began to
trade with people from
China and other Asian nations. Then, in 1521,
Ferdinand Magellan arrived in the Philippines on
an expedition from Spain. In 1565, more Spanish
people settled on the islands. Spain ruled the
Philippines until 1898. In August 1898, the United
States took control.

In 1946, the Philippines became independent. Between 1965 and 1986, the islands were ruled by a dictator named Ferdinand Marcos. Then a **revolution** put Corazon Aquino in power. She brought many changes to the Philippines.

Corazon Aquino

Callao Man

In 2007, archaeologists found a small bone in Callao Cave in Luzon. The bone was from a man who died about sixty-seven thousand years earlier. Callao Man is the first known person to live in the Philippines.

The Philippines is a **democracy**. Its government has three parts, or branches: the executive branch, the legislative branch, and the judicial branch.

President Rodrigo Duterte during a visit to Singapore in 2016.

The president leads the executive branch. He or she is elected every six years. The Philippines's president chooses advisors to be in his or her cabinet. Each cabinet member runs a part of the government.

The legislative branch makes the laws. It is called the Congress of the Philippines.

FACT!

The Philippines is divided into seventeen regions. Each region is governed by a council. Regions are divided into provinces. Each province has its own capital city.

The Congress has two parts: the House of Representatives and the Senate. The House of Representatives has more than two hundred members. The Senate has twenty-four members.

The judicial branch is made up of the Supreme Court. The Supreme Court and lower courts make sure laws are followed.

The Capital City

Manila is the capital city of the Philippines. More than 1.6 million people live there. It is the most densely populated city in the world.

The Economy

The Philippines has a strong **economy**. It is one of the strongest economies in East Asia. Many jobs make up the Philippines's economy. Some people work in stores, hotels, banks, restaurants, and businesses. Others are teachers, doctors, and government workers.

A young man makes clothes in a tailor shop in Quezon City.

In the past, **agriculture** made up most of the nation's economy. Today, about one-third of Filipinos work in agriculture. Rice and corn are the most popular foods to grow. The Philippines also sends sugar and coconuts to other parts of the world.

Transportation is also an important industry. There are many ways to travel the country. Few Filipinos own cars. Instead, they use public buses and trains. Boats called ferries carry people from island to island.

Philippine pesos

Pretty Money

Philippine money is called the peso. Pesos have images of famous Filipinos and come in many different colors.

The Environment

The Philippines has many beautiful places. The nation's rain forests are filled with giant fig trees and lauan trees, and a vine called rattan. Mangrove trees grow by the coast. These trees have long roots that rise out of the water.

A tarsier peers from a tree branch in a Philippine park.

Many different mammals live in the Philippines. Some, like the water buffalo, are very large. Others, like the tarsier, are small. The nation also has more than 50 kinds of bats and about 270 kinds of reptiles.

There are many different bird species on the islands. The Philippine eagle is the national bird. Other birds include cockatoos, hawks, ducks, and owls.

The waters around the Philippines are filled with life! Some examples include sharks, eels, lionfish, dolphins, and starfish.

A Reef Called Home

The Tubbataha Reef is home to over six hundred species of fish.

Fish swim in the Tubbataha Reef

Over 102 million people live in the Philippines. Filipinos belong to about one hundred different ethnic groups. The two largest groups are the Tagalogs and the Cebuano Visayans. Most Tagalogs live in or around Manila. Visayans live in the middle of the country.

A Tagalog family poses on a wooden walkway near their home.

About half of the people in the Philippines live in cities.

Other ethnic groups in the Philippines include Moros, Tausugs, Yakans, and Samals. The nation is also home to some ethnic Chinese. There is also a small population of Americans, Indians, Japanese, and Arabs.

Social Classes

The Philippines has three different social classes. The top social class makes up only 0.1 percent of the population. They have a lot of wealth and power. The middle class has stable jobs. One-quarter of all households are very poor. Sadly, some people live in garbage dumps such as Smokey Mountain or Payatas.

Lifestyle

Many people in the Philippines live in cities. Philippine cities are very crowded and noisy. City people live in apartments or small houses.

A Filipino family enjoys a day in the park in Quezon City.

Other people making up the Philippines's population live in villages in the country or along the coast. Country homes are often made of wood and palm leaves. Houses near the water are built on tall poles so they will stay dry.

FACT!

Many Filipinos live in extended families.

Filipino Weddings

Most Filipinos get married in a Catholic church. Muslim families are married by a religious leader called an imam.

A Filipino couple celebrates their marriage in a church.

Children must go to elementary school from ages seven to thirteen. After elementary school, many teenagers go to a secondary school for four years. Most Filipinos go to college after that. Other Filipinos go to work after elementary school. They may work in stores or shops. Teenagers that live in the country may work on family farms.

Religion

Most Filipinos are Roman Catholic. The Spanish brought Catholicism to the Philippines during the 1500s. **Missionaries** taught the faith to native people. Today, more than 80 percent of Filipinos

San Agustin Church in Manila

are Catholic. They celebrate traditional Catholic holidays, including Christmas, Easter, and the feast days of different saints.

Just over 11 percent of Filipinos belong to Christian churches. The Philippine Independent

FACT!

A small number of Filipinos are Hindus, Buddhists, or Baha'i.

Church is the most popular. It was started in 1902. Other Christian churches include Iglesia ni Cristo, the United Church of Christ, and the United Pentecostal Church.

These stone statues decorate a temple in the Philippines.

About 5 percent of the Philippines's population is Muslim. Muslim Filipinos are called Moros. Most live in Mindanao and other southern islands.

Different Gods

Some Filipinos practice split Christianity. It mixes Christian and ancient beliefs. People might pray to their ancestors or to the gods of rain or good harvest.

Language

People in the Philippines speak more than one hundred languages. They include Tagalog, Cebuano, Ilocano, Bicolano, and Samarnon. People in different parts of the country speak different languages.

Students enjoy their lessons in a Philippines classroom.

A New Alphabet

Long ago, Tagalog was written in an alphabet called Baybayin. The Spanish introduced their alphabet to the Philippines. Today, the Tagalog alphabet has twenty-eight letters.

FACT!

The Philippines is the third-largest English-speaking nation in the world.

The Philippines has two official languages. They are English and Filipino. Filipino is based on the Tagalog language.

Students learn English and Filipino in school. English is used in business and the government. Classes at universities are usually taught in English.

In the past, Filipino students had to learn Spanish in school. Many people still speak a little Spanish. Some Chinese people in the Philippines speak Fujianese or Hokkien.

The people of the Philippines create many different forms of art. Traditional crafts include weaving, woodcarving, and basket making. People in Cebu create beautiful art out of shells. Another traditional craft is making and painting pottery.

Musicians perform during a festival celebrating Earth Hour in 2015.

Lea Salonga is a famous actress and singer who comes from the Philippines.

Festivals for All

All Filipino towns hold festivals. Some festivals celebrate Catholic saints and traditions. Others celebrate ancient folk traditions.

Painting religious figures or scenes was very popular during the time that the Spanish ruled the Philippines. Later, painters showed native people in traditional clothes.

Music is a very important part of Filipino life. People enjoy many kinds of music, including rock and jazz. Many people attend concerts or play music at home. Other Filipinos enjoy dancing.

Filipino literature includes many themes of freedom and struggle. Literature was one of the ways the people fought for their independence from Spain and, later, the United States.

Fun and Play

People in the Philippines enjoy many different sports. Basketball is one of the most popular sports. Many children enjoy playing in public courts or in school. Other popular sports include golf, tennis, boxing, volleyball, and badminton.

Filipinos enjoy a basketball game.

The Philippine National Games

The Philippine National Games are held every year. Events include gymnastics, running, swimming, volleyball, and polo.

Jai alai is another popular sport. Players tie small baskets to their arms. They throw a ball from these baskets against a wall. Then the other player must throw it back.

Teams compete in sports such as soccer in the National Games.

Martial arts are popular in the Philippines. Many boys learn an art called arnis. Players try to knock each other over with long sticks. Both boys and girls play a game called *sipa*. Sipa is like volleyball, but players can only hit the ball with their knees and feet.

The Philippine Basketball Association is the oldest professional basketball league outside of the United States. It began in 1975.

Food

Rice is the most popular and important food in the Philippines. Every meal includes rice. It can be boiled or fried. Sometimes it is baked into cakes. A common meal in the Philippines is rice served with fish or meat. Vegetables such as beans or cabbage are also eaten with rice. So are fruits like bananas, mangoes, and

Chicken adobo over rice

FACT!

Drinks like mango shakes and coconut juice are very popular.

pineapples. Children enjoy a drink made of rice mixed with hot chocolate.

Adobo is a popular Filipino dish. Adobo is a sauce made of vinegar, soy sauce, and garlic. It is served over chicken, pork, beef, or vegetables.

Filipinos enjoy American restaurants as well as Filipino ones.

Food from Around the World

Many cultures introduced their foods to the Philippines. The Spanish brought paella and other dishes. The Chinese brought noodles, spring rolls, and buns filled with sweet bean paste. Americans brought hamburgers and other popular foods.

Glossary

agriculture   Farming.

democracy   A form of government in which people choose their leaders in elections.

economy   A system of goods or services that help make a country successful.

ethnic   Related to people who have a common national or cultural tradition.

missionaries   People who are sent by a religious group to teach that group's faith.

revolution   A violent movement by people to change their system of government.

terraces   Raised, flat platforms of land with steep sides.

Find Out More

Books

Burgan, Michael. *Philippines*. Chicago, IL:
    Heinemann Library, 2012.

Longworth, Holly. *The Philippines*. New York:
    Bearport Publishing, 2016.

Website

National Geographic Kids: Philippines

http://kids.nationalgeographic.com/explore/

countries/philippines/#philippines-island.jpg

Video

Family FUN in the Philippines

https://www.youtube.com/watch?v=29WkCdi8DU0

This video features a variety of different family

activities in the Philippines.

Index

About the Author

Joanne Mattern is the author of more than 250 books for children. She specializes in writing nonfiction and has explored many different places in her writing. Her favorite topics include history, travel, sports, biography, and animals. Mattern lives in New York State with her husband, four children, and several pets.